Little
Book of

Geeks

Luke Kirk

Crombie Jardine
PUBLISHING LIMITED

13 Nonsuch Walk, Cheam, Surrey, SM2 7LG
www.crombiejardine.com

Published by Crombie Jardine Publishing Limited
First edition, 2005

ISBN 1-905102-27-5

Written by Iain McAllister
Cartoons by Caitlin Urquhart
Designed by www.glensaville.com
Printed & bound in the United Kingdom by
William Clowes Ltd, Beccles, Suffolk

CONTENTS

INTRODUCTION

Welcome to the Hidden World

Throughout society's history, right up to the modern day, we have had a need to classify people: put them in groups so that we feel that we know how to approach, talk to or interact with a given individual. In the past this was merely working, middle and upper class, but as time went on, more and more classifications came to find a place within our language.

In recent times the phenomenon of the Chav, Ned or Schemie is well documented along with their middle class equivalent, the Goth. We label people Yobs, Yahs and Yuppies but there is one sub-class that is harder to identify. We all know they exist but it is not always obvious if you are talking to one of them, if your friend is one or even if you are one yourself. I refer, of course, to Geeks.

What Do We Mean by Geek?

Before we venture any further into the hidden world of Geeks, like explorers in a David Attenborough documentary, we must first do our research. Let us begin by looking at how to define what we mean by Geek.

Geek: A person who is socially uncomfortable or unfashionable, an obsessive enthusiast.

So we can see that Geek is a term used to define someone

obsessed with a particular thing, whether that be Star Wars, Star Trek, computer programming or their local football team.

Historically Geeky

Since the beginning of recorded history the Geek sub-class has been a part of all sections of society. However the original Geeks, and the ones whom the phrase was coined for, were circus performers who would carry out bizarre and outlandish tricks on stage, like biting the heads of chickens. Applying this to the modern day is obviously slightly out of context but we could happily label Ozzy Osbourne a Geek, albeit from hundreds of yards away, through a megaphone.

PERCEPTION OF GEEKS

Before we pull out our big book of Geeks and go off distinguishing the science-fiction nutballs from the fantasy fighters, let's have a little think about how the public perceive Geeks, and how Geeks actually are.

The Public Perception

The public view of the Geek is not exactly favourable. We imagine them as overweight, unhygienic, smelly, utterly obsessed with one thing in particular, socially awkward and lacking in any kind of oratorical skill. Their obsessions usually manifest themselves outside what most would see as healthy pursuits of normal people, like watching Coronation Street and reality TV programmes or talking about house prices, and descend into the far murkier depths of science fiction, Buffy worship, prancing about in costumes pretending to be other people, or trying to get 100% completion on the latest video game before anyone else can claim the victory.

The Reality

Much as Geeks would like to
think the public is misguided in
its opinion, there is some truth in
its outlook. A large percentage
of Geeks *do* tend to be, in one
way or another, unhygienic,
socially awkward and have weird
obsessions they will prattle on
about for hours. However,
recalling our definition of Geek,
we can see that it could be quite
easy to classify ardent football

fans, or those with an obsession for cars and gadgets or even a predilection for modern music, as geeky. To this end, from here on I will refer to the public perception of Geeks as PP.

A GUIDE TO GEEK SPOTTING

Classification

Geeks come in many shapes, sizes, smells, colours and - more importantly - interests. Our dictionary definition leads us to the conclusion that anyone with an obsession about anything can be happily classified as a Geek. However when we refer to PP Geeks we usually mean they have specific interests that allow us to label them as weird, unusual and unsociable. It is these members

of the Geek species that we will
concentrate on for now in the
hope of being able to identify and
interact with such an interesting
sub-class of the human race.

Sci-Fi Geeks

The most easily identifiable of all Geeks, the science-fiction members tend to be either very thin or incredibly large and happily display symbols of their favourite show or shows about their person. The most common type of science-fiction Geek is the ubiquitous Star Trek fan or 'Trekkie' whose fixation with the voyages of the USS Enterprise border on the psychotic. Proudly delivering lines of logic from Spock, fighting like Kirk or learning how to say their marriage vows in Klingon, these individuals believe that Star Trek can teach the world a thing or two about love and understanding. In fact some would claim that everything they know they learnt from Star Trek.

Of course it would be foolish to think that all Sci-Fi Geeks are Trekkies – far from it. Other favourite shows include: Babylon 5, Farscape, any of the new trek-based space adventures, which some Old Trek fans despise, and Dr.Who. In fact for any of the numerous science fiction shows of past and present you are going to be able to find at least one obsessive fan proudly standing akimbo in their living room displaying their Babylon 5 boxer shorts whilst waving a light sabre.

The predilection for sci-fi is not merely restricted to the small or silver screen however. Many Sci-Fi Geeks exist solely, or partly, as readers of vast swathes of science fiction, yet again enjoying quoting, as often as possible, pieces of wisdom from Asimov, Clarke and Adams.

Some particular favourites of this type are shown opposite. Watch out for any signs of these around your loved ones and then ask them the questions in the 'Are You a Geek?' section later in the book. This is a good way to start taking steps towards Geek acceptance.

1) Star Trek: To boldly seduce aliens that no one has seduced before.

2) Star Wars: Everyone wants to be Vader or the emperor.

3) Babylon 5: Boldly sitting around and waiting for something to happen.

4) Firefly: Don't mention that it only had one series. It's awesome - remember that.

5) Roswell: Dawson's Creek meets little green men.

6) Mutant X: It's like X-men only with far less budget.

7) Farscape: Better than Star Trek, just don't say that to a Trekkie. They get violent.

8) Dune: The mini series was better than the films is not an argument you want to start.

9) X-files: How can we confuse you? Let me count the ways.

Fantasy Geeks

Lovers of all things magical, mystical and heroic, these

members of the Geek family are often mistaken for the science-fiction variety just described, due to their similar appearance and habitats. However their interests represent a polar opposite to the scientific obsessions of their cousins. They will think nothing of reading several thousand-page novels, each one identical in plot and characters to the last, but all detailing the adventures of their favourite hero/heroine.

They also love nothing more than reading a series of books about fantastical worlds - no matter how badly written those books may be.

Lord of the Rings tends to be the book or film of choice and there are those who can speak, sing and write in Elfish and Dwarfish. Arguments frequently break out between Tolkien lovers and those who would insist on pointing out that Gandalf could have solved all their problems earlier by summoning his gigantic eagle friends (the bastard).

Fantasy Geeks tend to have a particular love of dragons and large mythical beasts and also have a tendency to believe strongly in mystical rituals, healing stones and the like.

As with the Sci-Fi Geeks, this group has its own particular favourites:

1) Lord of the Rings: Everyone has a favourite character. Don't declare yours till they

have declared theirs; it could lead to much conflict and unwanted debate.

2) Discworld: It's like every other fantasy world only flatter and funnier.

3) Anne Mcaffrey and her dragon novels: Lots of bloody dragons.

4) Any books set in the worlds of Warhammer and Warhammer 40'000: A crossover with the RPG war-gaming

crowd but still popular.

5) David Eddings:
   Really big books.

6) JK Rowling: For all
   generations. Apparently.

7) George RR Martin:
   Conspiracy-laden
   fantasy that gets
   confusing as the X-files.

Computer Geeks

This classification actually covers two members of the Geek family: Computer

Gamers and Computer Nerds. The former are those who live and breathe computer games, thinking nothing of spending hours entrenched in virtual worlds interacting with other gamers, or just with the AI (artificial intelligence) of the game in question. Computer Nerds are more practical than their Gamer cousins, but no less obsessed. They are the programmers, IT experts and Microsoft- and Mac-obsessed people most of us have met during our lives. They spend hours attached to computer screens reprogramming their favourite games, writing their own programmes and having fights online with people who don't think Linux, Mac or Microsoft are any good, depending on their own preferences.

Science Geeks

Certainly the most practical-minded of the Geek species, these tend to be found exclusively in research facilities, universities, libraries or the local 'academic drinking house'. This type comes in several different forms - all of them found within their own sections of the aforementioned buildings: chemists, physicists, biologists, mathematicians, the list goes on and on, and is too long by far to include in this short treatise on the subject.

Scientists are the hardest to identify of the Geek groups, their behaviour, seemingly withdrawn, is otherwise normal unless one touches upon their subject of choice, at which point they will display their livery and charge full force into the social gathering to show their prowess.

Comic Book Geeks

Despite being very similar to their Sci-Fi and Fantasy cousins, Comic Book Geeks are worth a mention if only to include their places of worship in the habitats section to follow. Usually possessors of enough paper to make rainforest conservationists fall to their knees and weep, this Geek sub-class will get stressed and irritated if denied the next installment of their comic of choice.

The interest in superheroes displayed in the cinemas these days has led to a resurgence of this type of Geek, long thought to be on the decline. The Comic Book Geek's particular favourites are:

1) X-Men: They're mutants and they're here to save the world.

2) Spiderman: He's a lovelorn teenager with the powers of spider!

3) Constantine: He smokes a lot

and kicks demonic ass.

4) Hellboy: He smokes a
   lot, is a demon and kicks
   lots of ass.

5) Sandman: Neil Gaman's,
   Magna Opus. The king of
   dreams has a hard time and
   has to choose between life
   and death. It also gave rise
   to a spin off.

6) Lucifer: Having given
   up on Hell, Satan goes
   and becomes God in his
   own universe.

7) Transmetropolitan: Gonzo journalist brings down the man.

8) Sin City: Things get ugly in a noir world where it's not all black and white.

9) Warren Ellis: Not a book but one of the recognized storytelling gods in the comic world.

10) Preacher: Man goes and hunts down God to hold him to account for the world being so shitty.

Twitcher Geeks

A relatively recent explosion in bird watching and bird watchers has led to society coming across this rather specialized type of Geek. They seek out and spot, or preferably photograph, birds that are not where they should be: namely birds from other countries that are rarely seen on these shores. So prevalent is this phenomenon becoming that occasionally articles will appear on local news channels relating to the location of a particularly rare bird in the area.

The people (mostly men, it has to be said) who engage in this activity tend to be upper-class or fairly well off middle-class citizens, who can afford to bunk off work whenever they like and jet about the country looking for rare bird life. A recent addition to the hobby seems to be to gather together near the sight of a rare bird and talk loudly about how they have digiscoped the bird: captured it in their very expensive digital telescopes.

Roleplayer Geeks

Most of the Geek types we have looked at, with the possible exception of the Twitchers, also cross into this category. That is not to say that all Fantasy, Computer, Sci-Fi and Science Geeks *are* also Roleplayers. For those who are unfamiliar with the hobby it is basically Cowboys and Indians with rules. Roleplayers refer to it as 'interactive storytelling', and that is a fairly good analogy. One group of Geeks, called Players, interacts with a world and story prepared by another Geek, called the Games Master, or GM, using a set of rules to determine the outcome of any actions taken within that imaginary world.

There are some non-Geek people who do this, but these members of the Geek family tend to be incredibly invested in the people they portray in these fantasy worlds, normally referred to as Player Characters, or PCs. They have continuous fights between each other over which set of rules is best, who portrays their character the best and how they can get the most out of the rules, sometimes referred to as being Munchkins. Their conversations tend to revolve around what fantastic thing their character did last session (which is a period of participating in a roleplaying game). They will also bombard their favourite game designers with annoying questions and irritating details about their character and think nothing of talking about their characters to non-Roleplayers, whether those individuals want to listen to them or not.

As with some of the previous types we have discussed there are many worlds for a Roleplayer to indulge in, a few of the favourites being:

1) World of Darkness: Vampires, werewolfs and wraiths, oh my!

2) Warhammer Fantasy Roleplay: Does exactly what it says on the tin.

3) Call of Cthulu: Squibbly horrible things that make you go mad.

4) Deadlands: This may be the Wild West but I've got a ray gun.

5) Dungeons & Dragons: Hit

things. Get treasure. Wash, rinse and repeat.

6) Paranoia: Don't worry about getting killed – you have plenty of clones.

7) Hero: The superhero system allowing you to create anything you want, as long as you have the super computer needed to do the calculations.

8) 7th Sea: Arrggh, pirates, lad.

Uber-Geeks

A more knowledgeable, and
usually larger and intimidating,
member of the Geek family,
the Uber-Geek is the ultimate
expression of the PP view.
Towering above all other
Geeks, proclaiming their
knowledge behind the safety
of an internet sign-on, these
individuals live and breathe
their hobbies, even more than
a normal Geek does. Some
Geeks revere them, others
berate them but everyone

fears coming across one when in a conversation about their specialist subject. Beware the Uber-Geek.

Other Geeks

Of course this selection is just the tip of the iceberg, and it would be possible to write many volumes on the other members of the Geek family. Our earlier definition allows for the descriptions of hundreds of different types of Geek, one for every hobby you can possibly imagine. Suffice to say that Geek interests are wide and varied and there will always be something new coming along that will have its zealots and obsessive patrons creating its own group of followers and Geeks.

Markings

The markings of most Geeks are very similar from one type to the next. However, there are two distinct modes of dress for Geeks: casual and smart. Casual dress consists of jeans, t-shirt and trainers, and usually a long coat or short jacket. Normally the t-shirt will have some kind of logo on it declaring the Geek's affiliation, but be assured that it is not always possible for a Geek to be identified purely by clothing. The smart Geek has a tendency to be a Roleplayer or a Fantasy type. They will wear very smart, if outdated, clothing on a regular basis, often wearing a trilby or other

old hat, and maybe sporting
something like a cane or other
old-fashioned accessory.

Identification

Markings are one thing, but
identifying Geeks through their
overall appearance can be
a much better place to start.
They have a tendency not
to wash on a regular basis,
often displaying a greasy, long
mane of hair. Their smell can
be quite distinct and when
they gather together it can

be overpowering to those not used to such pungent odours. The well-dressed specimens described earlier tend to be very well kept, better so than their average counterparts, and would be able to fool most people if it weren't for their mode of dress.

Behavioural Patterns

All members of the Geek family have very similar behavioural patterns. They are completely obsessed with whatever it is they have taken an interest in and will expound its virtues at every possibility. Their behaviour can be unsettling and disturbing to those not used to handling this family of human. To be trapped in a conversation with a Geek about their obsession can be a disconcerting experience as they try to stop you from leaving so they can elaborate on just one more point.

However, not all Geeks behave in this anti-social way. Some

keep their hobbies under wraps unless the conversation particularly turns towards it. Others will deny their obsession even exists, preferring to remain in the Geek closet as it were, refusing to expose themselves to the ridicule that may ensue should they 'come out.' The majority of 'outed' Geeks feel some anger towards these closet Geeks but in some cases it can be necessary not to reveal every facet of their lives to their colleagues. There are certain professions that would happily mock those with interests outside what would be deemed as acceptable by their peers, and the consequences can be more than just personal.

TO BE OR NOT TO BE... A GEEK

Before discussing where one can find and talk to Geeks, I would like to touch on one slightly controversial area of Geek culture. We have already looked at the definition of Geek, touching upon the PP Geek types that exist. Let us take a moment to look at socially acceptable geekiness – and indeed perhaps ourselves. Do you, or your loved one have an obsession with a football team? Do you watch the Grand Prix, Top Gear, wax your car every other day and cover your house with bike and car magazines? Do you travel to other countries to pursue these interests? If so, sorry guys and girls, you're Geeks.

Nothing to be ashamed of, and it is a source of pride for thousands, if not millions, across the world, but you have probably never thought of yourself in this way. If you are unsure whether you are a Geek or not at this point then please refer to the 'Are You a Geek?' section later in the book, as this includes advice on what to do if you discover you are a Geek.

Natural Habitats

Geeks seem to have an innate ability to seek out and locate other Geeks. A kind of pack instinct takes over when they want to find like-minded souls. Different sub-classes obviously gather in different places, but there will always be somewhere in a given city where you can find enclaves of Geeks. For Roleplayers it will be the local gaming society or games shop; for Comic Book Geeks, the local comic book shop; for

Sci-Fi Geeks, the local cinema and book club etc. These clubs are repositories of very specific knowledge and usually advertize their presence to others through posters, so tracking down and observing Geeks is usually fairly easy.

Although these places do advertize themselves to fellow Geeks, if you are in a town that has no such meeting places, or they are in the process of being established, they can be hard to track down. In this instance it is necessary to rely on word of mouth, meaning you will need to pass yourself off as a Geek to gain information, or try talking to normal people in the town to find where the local Geek depository is. If you go down the most desperate route of just wandering about town until you find a place of Geek worship, then keep an eye out down small, out-of-the-way back streets, as these tend to breed 'specialist' shops much in the same way as a teenage boy develops acne.

Conventions

One other habitat worth mentioning is the 'Convention', a gathering of people, (mainly Geeks) who all share the same interest or hobby, meeting in order to participate in that pastime. The most commonly known type of convention leads us back to the Sci-Fi sub-class: the Trekkie. Here fans of the show meet to discuss their problems with different episodes, to meet their heroes, get photos signed and generally dress up and look a bit stupid.

Most Geek conventions mirror these, though dressing up only tends to occur at Sci-Fi, Fantasy and Roleplaying conventions. All conventions consist of events and seminars on various topics relevant to the Geeks attending and most will be able to conjure up a special guest or two. The smaller conventions may only be able to get security guard no.2 from episode 35 of whatever show it is, but the bigger conventions enjoy the privilege of having Kirk himself and his buddies, or the equivalent, turn up, sign photos and try to look happy answering irritating questions.

Approaching and Interacting with Geeks

Techniques for approaching and talking to Geeks vary slightly from species to species, but the basic principles always remain the same. The first task for any would-be Geek spotter is to find places of Geek worship. Those of you who have been paying attention will now know that these places are not particularly difficult to find, as they tend to advertize their presence to fellow Geeks.

One of the easiest ways to interact with Geeks is to become one, or at least pretend to become one, yourself. Here are my top five tips for becoming, or at least seeming to become, a Geek.

1) Make your hobby an obsession

Pick something you enjoy doing in your spare time and fixate on it. Learn all you can about it, paying particular attention to obscure facts that very few people would know.

2) Find the local association for your hobby and join it

Find out if there is a local

society for your hobby and join it. If there is not a local society then you will gain admiration from your fellow Geeks by setting up one and declaring yourself 'El Presidente'.

3) Go to a convention for your hobby with fellow Geeks

There are conventions and gatherings for nearly every single hobby imaginable. Go to yours. Take photos. Show them to your loved ones and parents who don't really care or understand.

4) Talk about your hobby to people who could not care less about it

Bring up your hobby in conversations whenever you can, even if they are about something else altogether. Butt in whenever other people are talking to mention this great thing that happened in Star Trek or during your last roleplaying session.

5) Indoctrinate someone into your hobby who has no interest in your hobby

The ultimate challenge for any would-be Geek is to make someone else a Geek, even if they didn't want to be in the first place. It is a subtle art that requires some practice, but with dedication and diligence even the most stalwart opponent can be indoctrinated!

Following these steps, you will be well on your way

to becoming the irritating obsessive that society likes to classify as a Geek.

Engaging a Geek

Now that you have some idea of what it takes to become a Geek, and you have found your targets, be it one solitary Geek away from his pack, or a rampaging horde of them bathing in the worship of their hobby, there are some definite do's and don'ts when actually engaging with Geeks.

Do

- Wear clothes proclaiming your Geek status.

- Open the conversation by asking about the latest thing in your hobby; this will single you out as someone who knows what they are talking about, and will also allow identification of the most knowledgeable Geek, or 'Alpha male', in the pack.

- Approach Geeks in their natural habitat. This shows

you have found out where the
local club for their hobby is,
which they will respect.

- Mention the internet forums
  you have joined or websites
  you have found relating to
  the hobby.

Don't

- Overstep your knowledge.
  If you are discovered as a
  fraud it may be hard to
  regain their trust.

- Question the knowledge of a

Geek, unless you have
firm evidence to back up
your question.

- Try to invite your new Geek
  friends to something 'normal'
  until you know them better;
  they may be scared of non-
  Geek contact.

- Say you have a girlfriend
  (even if you do); they may
  find it intimidating or annoying
  that you get sex and they
  don't, and aren't likely to any
  time soon.

Generic Geek Favourites

It would be easy to conclude the findings so far by saying that all Geeks are different in some way or another whether due to obsession or how they act out that obsession. However there are some things that draw Geeks together: oppression, being suspicious of normal people, the chance of sex, and films and music. For some reason Geeks tend to like very similar types of music and films, and for a sake of completeness I provide a few examples here. If you like say 70% of the items on these lists please take the 'Are You a Geek?' test on p.89.

Films

1) Donnie Darko

2) Fear & Loathing in Las Vegas

3) Matrix

4) Star Wars

5) Ghostbusters

6) Groundhog Day

7) Big Lebowski

8) Dogma

9) Memento

10) Monty Python films

Music

1) DJ Shadow

2) Radiohead

3) Queen

4) Jimi Hendrix

5) Mr. Scruff

6) Classical music (all types)

7) Royskopp

8) Jazz, especially Louis Armstrong and Ella Fitzgerald

9) Swing, especially Frank Sinatra

10) Soundtracks picked because the director or the film is a favourite.

Geek Uses Within Society

Although the 'normal' people within society may deride and

ridicule Geeks, Geeks are actually an incredibly useful section of the population. From helping us to win the local pub quiz with an obscure question about Princess Lea's bra size, to fixing our home computers, Geeks find themselves both needed and shunned at the same time. Nevertheless, the use of Geeks within society can provide us with a very interesting point to start from when wishing to track and identify Geeks.

Pub Quizzes

Pubs. A strange mix of a centre of Geek worship, and prime Geek-spotting territory, the local pub quizzes in **every** town in Britain, and probably the world, are great places for normal people to approach and interact with all types of Geek. It is an easy point to make that those who have an obsession with general knowledge are Geeks themselves, but that is by the by.

Most pub quiz teams will have at least one Geek in them, usually specializing in a general area like films, books, TV etc rather than the more specific ones we have discussed before. These Geeks often have interests that are more on the fringe of social acceptability, and so are good starting points for anyone wishing to interact with Geeks, as they tend to be fairly normal on the surface.

Geeks as Repositories of Knowledge

If you can track down the right Geeks, they can be very useful sources of knowledge. So obsessed is a Geek with his particular interest that it is sometimes easier to track down the one you want and ask them questions, than trawl through the mire of information that a library or the internet can provide you with.

Geeks in Business

Many different types of businesses use Geeks and in fact some companies actively seek out and employ Geeks, especially those firms concerned with the computer and IT industry. Since our society is now so inextricably tied to technology, it's a simple matter to see that we are all in some way indebted to a Geek for our e-mail, phone etc. somewhere along the line.

Geeks are also helpful in retail businesses: we rely on them to inform us about computer products, DVDs, the latest music, which wine is best with salmon etc. Never underestimate the usefulness of a Geek, and never forget that you might not know you are talking to one.

ARE YOU A GEEK?

So we have defined what a Geek is, and identified a few of the many types that exist in the world. You are possibly even now coming to the conclusion that you yourself are a Geek, that your hobby is an obsession and that you have an unhealthy and 'Geeky' interest or hobby. Let's break down the behaviour of Geeks so that you can ask yourself a few questions and find out whether you are indeed a Geek or not...

1) Do you have a hobby (hobbies)? By hobby, read an interest you pursue in your spare time. This could be anything from cinema attendance, DVD watching, reading books etc.

2) Do you engage in your hobby whenever possible? I.e. If you have spare time do you try and engage in one or all of your hobbies, before anything else?

3) Do you talk about your

hobby with other people who are interested in it, whenever you get the chance?

4) Do you try to get your hobby into conversations even if the conversation has nothing to do with your hobby?

5) Do you start conversations about your hobby before anything else if no conversation is currently running?

6) Does your hobby occupy your idle thoughts?

7) Will you travel to other areas of the country to engage in your hobby? (Yes, that includes football matches, guys.)

8) Will you travel to other countries to engage in your hobby? (Yep, football matches again.)

9) Will you regularly, say one day in two, wear clothes or items on your person that would indicate your hobby to the rest of the world?

10)Is a large percentage of
   your possessions connected
   to your hobby?

**So how many did you answer in
the affirmative?**

Yes to 0-3: You have a hobby
you like to engage in but you
wouldn't try and talk to every
stranger in the street about it,
nor would you try and shove
it down the throats of anyone
who didn't care about it. You're
definitely not a Geek.

Yes to 4-6: You have a hobby,

or hobbies, you like to
engage in whenever you have
a spare moment and enjoying
talking about it with people
who are interested in the same
thing or want to find out more
about it. You don't bring it up
all the time in conversations but
do try to whenever it seems
appropriate. You're a Geek,
a nice one, a mild one, but a
Geek all the same.

Yes to 7-10: You have an
obsession, not a hobby and
everyone should love your

hobby. EVERYONE! You see nothing wrong with spending hundreds if not thousands of pounds on your hobby and will happily travel to other parts of your own country as well as others to pursue your favourite writers, actors, teams, etc. You are most definitely a Geek, possibly an Uber-Geek.

If you have discovered that you are a Geek during this questionnaire, then I urge you not to worry. It is possible to continue life as a Geek, though the road

can be hard and fraught with
self-doubt, ridicule and humiliation.
Rest assured though, that there
are other Geeks out there who
will embrace you into their dark,
dingy circles of worship, where
you can truly learn and appreciate
what it is to be a Geek. I myself
have met many well-adjusted
and sociable individuals who are
Geeks beneath the surface. They
have jobs, attend concerts, go
to the pub and lead normal lives.
DON'T PANIC. The first thing to
do is tell your loved ones. Their

reaction may be one of
shock and worry at first but
eventually they will come to
accept your hobby and may even
support you in pursuing it. Your
friends will also be shocked by
the revelation but will stick by
you, if they are true friends. You
can, and should, lead a normal life
post-Geek revelation.

RELATIONSHIPS

It would be easy to think that Geeks are so anti-social and withdrawn that they are totally incapable of forming relationships with anyone, and for some this is indeed, sadly, true. However, just like normal people, the majority of Geeks are perfectly capable of interacting with others, even if those people don't actually want to interact with them. We will look at two different types of relationships, Inter- and Extra-Geek relationships, from

the point of view of platonic
relationships, friendships, and
sexual relationships. Yes, Geeks
do sometimes get lucky and
indulge in sex.

Please note that for sexual
relationships I am talking about
male-female relationships.
This is not say that Geek
sexual relationships are strictly
hetero, but the majority certainly
seem to be and therefore this is
the area of greatest interest in
this short guide.

Inter-Geek Relationships

These are the types of relationships that involve two, or more, Geeks. Not all, or both, of the Geeks in an Inter-Geek relationship need to have the same interests, and it is quite common to find groups of Geeks that contain many of the types we have discussed already.

Platonic

Platonic relationships between Geeks are common and encouraged, especially by worried parents who think their little Geek will never have any friends, let alone partners. These friendships are usually formed purely by accident, when one Geek finds another like-minded individual by chance, but also emerge from the quagmire of geekiness that can be found at University clubs and the like. Their friendships tend to revolve around their shared hobby at first: inviting each other over to play video games etc, but over time evolve into as normal a friendship as the average man in the street engages in with his beer buddies.

Sexual

Let's face it, the majority of Geeks tend to be men, because men seem more likely to have strange little hobbies like sci-fi watching, roleplaying, fanatically polishing their cars etc. Thus when a woman starts to engage in a similar hobby, the males of the species will gather around her like flies to a corpse. The males will show off 'Geek bravado' by demonstrating precisely how much more they know than the other Geeks, a kind of mental arm wrestling if you will. Some females become distressed by this behaviour and will gravitate towards the quieter members of the pack who have not been hassling them. Alternatively they'll simply run. Others find it very flattering and will manipulate the males within a group to get who and what they want.

Long-term inter-Geek relationships tend to be few and far between, and females within a Geek pack sometimes have a tendency to change partners many times over the lifetime of their involvement in the pack.

Extra-Geek Relationships

Of course Geeks do not purely interact with other Geeks, and it is quite normal to find non-Geeks, or 'normal' people, and Geeks in each other's company. The Geeks who are best at this are the ones who, at first glance, appear reasonably normal and well dressed, only to have their Geek obsession lurking just below the surface of the skin.

Platonic

Most of the time initial contact with people will not be enough to tell straight away that someone is a Geek. The ones who advertize themselves as Star Wars fans etc. are of course fairly easy to identify as Geeks, and they tend to find it harder to make friends with non-Geeks. Most extra-Geek relationships are started before the non-Geek realizes the other person is a Geek. Once the friendship is formed and the Geek and non-Geek are getting on well together, then the Geek's obsession will come out and most non-Geeks are happy to accept that their new friend happens to be a little bit obsessive in one area of their life. Some can't handle it, but in the end the majority of Geeks have friends who most people would regard as 'normal'.

Sexual

This happens more often than you might think, though a lot of non-Geek females can't really relate to a Geek's obsession. For some reason (and if someone can tell me why this is so, please contact me) women in general do not tend to invest as much time as men do in their spare time pursuits. Anyway, back to the point. These relationships do happen, and have the same successes and problems as any normal relationship. Both parties must be careful though: the non-Geek should respect the Geek's time needed to pursue his hobby, and the Geek will need to realize that spending all his spare time thinking about games, football, films etc, is not conducive to a healthy relationship. Take heed, Geeks and non-Geeks!

Geek Chat-Up Lines

Not known for style or social grace, Geeks have a difficult time approaching women and getting across the fact that they like a particular female. They generally manage this through displays of Geek bravado, the type of showing off usually reserved for the local club. Chat-up lines as such don't really exist but opening lines to a conversation that will

show off their geekiness and
hopefully attract potential Geek
mates may be as follows:

'Hey d'you know I have my
own space ship, saved the
galaxy and almost died saving
my friends? All in last night's
roleplaying session!'

'That's nothing - I once rolled
five 6s in a row.'

'Would you like to go and
see the new [insert movie
name here]? It won't be as
good as [insert movie name

here] but [insert long rambling explanation to show off Geek knowledge here]? Yeah, so would you like to...'

'Would you like to have dinner at the restaurant at the end of the universe?'

'I know the question to the ultimate answer.'

'I discovered this really cool bacteria last night....'

'Would you like to borrow that CD then, it's not as good as ...

[insert long rambling explanation to show off insane music knowledge] ... but I'll let you borrow it. Shall I come round and drop it off tomorrow?'

And so forth. Geeks are not good at picking up women, but somehow they still manage it, despite their lack of charm, hygiene or sophistication.

Giving Geek Gifts

There may come a time in your relationship with a Geek that you need to buy him or her a present or two, you know, for birthdays and that sort of thing. It can be a difficult task for non-Geeks to buy their geeky loved ones a present and so I provide a few tips should you be stuck for ideas.

Rule #1:

When in doubt, buy him or her a book of their favourite show, author, actor/actress, operating system etc It doesn't really matter if they have it already, it will make their collection look bigger thus boosting their status amongst fellow Geeks. I know people with 12 different versions of Lord of The Rings and another one never goes amiss.

Rule #2:

The majority of Geeks will own a computer or games system. Buy them something for it. Even better, buy something imported for it as this will make you look like you went to extra effort, even if you didn't, especially if it is something from Japan.

Rule #3:

A lot of Geeks have a particularly
favourite brand of liquor, most
of which will have obscure or
exclusive versions available. Find
it and buy it. Most cities will
have good wine merchants
where you would find this sort
of thing. Brandy, tequila and
bourbon are the most common
choices I have come across.

Rule #4:

If you happen to be in a physical
relationship with a Geek then

you may have noticed they get
a bit pungent at times and dress
badly. A can of industrial strength
deodorant or 'What not to wear!"
can be used as not so subtle hints
in the right direction.

Rule #5:

Good places to shop for Geeks
include Electronics Boutique,
Game, HMV, Games Workshop,
Waterstones, Virgin and the
Gadget Shop. Geeks love silly or
daft presents from these places
and don't forget a proportion of

the staff are probably Geeks of one type or another themselves.

Rule #6:

Tickets to a cheesy kung fu movie, cool sci-fi films, epic fantasy or innovative low budget films are always a good choice. DO NOT buy him tickets to the girly rom com you want to see: Geeks are usually romantics at heart, but never want to admit it.

Rule #7:

Geeks love gadgets of all shapes

and sizes, especially if they can
be used in an obscure way in their
hobby.   Buy a Roleplayer Geek
an electronic dice generator, get
a Sci-Fi Geek a Klingon translator,
etc - these sort of things go down
a treat. Just remember to hide
the batteries when you are fed
up of hearing 'Gimme some sugar
baby' translated into Klingon for
the 42nd time.

CONCLUSION

So what can you, the reader,
take from this little treatise?
What should be the final piece
of advice for you? Geeks are
people too. They have jobs and
lives outside their hobbies (apart
from the Uber-Geeks, of course)
but all in all they are as nice, or
as nasty, as any other people
you meet every day. In fact
it's entirely likely that you know
Geeks but had never realized.
Does Johnson talk about his car

too much during the tea break in the office? Does your boyfriend delay you going to the cinema to beat the last boss on Tomb Raider or does your boss have an annoyingly obsessive way of talking about celebrities? Geeks are a useful slice of society, so be careful next time you make fun of them as they may just help you fix your computer someday. Just don't ask them if they think PCs or Macs are better...

ISBN 1-905102-26-7

£2.99

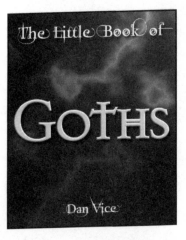

The Little Book of

GOTHS

Dan Vice

ISBN 1-905102-24-0

£2.99

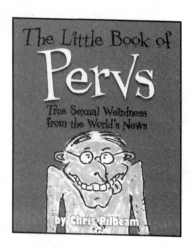

The Little Book of

Pervs

True Sexual Weirdness
from the World's News

by Chris Pilbeam

ISBN 1-905102-38-0

£2.99

ISBN 1-905102-28-3

£2.99

Are you or a friend a Geek?

Do you have any funny
Geek stories?

Tell us, we want to know
makeitso@crombiejardine.com

All Crombie Jardine books
are available from your High
Street bookshops, Amazon,
Littlehampton Book Services, or
Bookpost (P.O.Box 29, Douglas,
Isle of Man, IM99 1BQ.
tel: 01624 677 237,
email: bookshop@enterprise.net.
Free postage and packing within the UK).